上海的新标志，

A new symbol for Shanghai,

孕育于天时与地利。

rooted in time and place.

Produced by Gensler Publications

2101 Webster St., Suite 2000

Oakland, CA 94612 USA

www.gensler.com

Distributed by ORO editions

Publishers of Architecture, Art, and Design

www.oroeditions.com

ISBN: 978-1-935935-12-4

Library of Congress data is available on request.

10 9 8 7 6 5 4 3 2 1 First edition

Printed in China

Shanghai Tower

Contents

远大志向
High Aspirations

上海中心大厦不仅仅是一个超高层大楼。作为亚洲最高的建筑,上海中心象征着中国在全球如日中天的地位以及经济实力,也象征着中国的远大志向:一座中国投资打造的世界级建筑。上海中心大厦让中国人民和上海中心的租户都引以为荣。同时,业主也非常着重于开放大楼给来自世界各地各行各业的人共享。

现在大厦完工了,我们即此反思项目的深远意义。对于这般规模的项目,相信每个人的看法都不尽相同。但我相信大家都能同意这栋建筑是绝对创新的。上海中心的设计将超高层建筑提升到新境界,利用优化风阻的外围幕墙,来创造从底部到顶端的人性化空中大堂。

上海中心大厦也代表着社群意识。夏军是土生土长的上海人,从项目初始就带领着建筑团队,每当他谈到童年的石库门宅院时都特别感性。上海中心的设计便是采用这个概念,运用真实的社区空间,创造了垂直的邻里社区。总而言之,上海中心大厦无与伦比的魅力始终深深吸引我。塔楼螺旋向上的建筑语汇,诉说着上海在世界舞台上举足轻重的地位。上海转型成一个亮眼的国际化大都会,让市民对自己、这个城市和国家的卓越成就感到骄傲。上海中心大厦已然成为代表上海的新标志。

Art Gensler
创办人

Shanghai Tower is more than just a tall building. As Asia's tallest, it represents China and its rising position in the world as a social and economic power. It's also a tremendous symbol for the country's aspirations—a global project built with Chinese investment. The tower lends prestige to the people of China and the tenants who occupy it. But, at the same time, it was important to our client that the building be open and accessible to people from all walks of life.

Now that the tower is completed, we have a chance to reflect on its meaning. Many people will have their own views on this, but I think we can all agree that it's brilliantly innovative. It takes the idea of a supertall building to a new place—leveraging the outer façade, which sheds the wind, to create sky gardens that provide human-scaled places from bottom to top.

The tower is also about community. Jun Xia, the Shanghai native who led the design from the start, speaks like a poet when he recalls the features of the courtyard houses he knew as a child. Using the same planning concepts, Shanghai Tower creates vertical neighborhoods with true community spaces. Finally, I have to say I'm completely captivated by the sheer presence of Shanghai Tower. Its spiral form reflects Shanghai's place in the world, its transformation as a global metropolis, and the pride its citizens take in the accomplishments of their city and their nation. Now it's the new symbol of Shanghai.

Art Gensler
Founder

高耸入云的塔楼

The tower's sheer presence

象征着上海在世界的地位。

reflects Shanghai's place in the world.

设计
灵感

Design Inspiration

设计概念

设计上海中心这般具有象征性的建筑，是千载难逢的机会，设计方案必须要能令人耳目一新。设计团队用心观察上海市的肌理，希望在设计中反映出上海独有的特色：蜿蜒迤逦的黄埔江勾勒出的城市线条，和不对称布局带来的各种可能性。

大厦空间规划也体现了中国人生活中，缓冲室内与室外的"朦胧空间"，这是在上海特有的石库门建筑常见的元素，长长的里弄和庭院是上海社交生活的背景。上海中心设计将这种里弄的布局垂直呈现。

Design concepts

The extraordinary opportunity to design Shanghai Tower called for a solution that had never before been imagined. But what? We looked to the city and its neighborhoods for inspiration. Shaped by the curves of the Huangpu River, the layout of Shanghai is dynamic and asymmetrical—qualities we wanted the tower to embody.

We were also careful to take note of the Chinese people's affinity for indoor-outdoor living, a lifestyle reflected in the city houses known as *shikumen*, whose narrow alleys and courtyards are a canvas for social life. Shanghai Tower draws on this same planning concept, but applies it vertically rather than horizontally.

规划为陆家嘴金融中心的亮点, 位于高密度市区的上海中心必须克服许多外力挑战。圆三角柱形的形体和外立面的缓和曲线, 使得上海中心大厦和邻近高楼的棱角相辅相成。

金茂大厦、环球金融中心和上海中心大厦形成的三大塔楼, 分别象征上海的过去、现在、和未来, 上海中心大厦的完工也为25年前规划的陆家嘴超高层建筑群画下完美的句点。

Planned as the centerpiece of the city's Lujiazui financial district, Shanghai Tower mediates many forces that converge on the dense urban site. With its triangular footprint, rounded corners, and subtly curved façade, the tower complements the strong, sharp edges of neighboring buildings.

On an urban scale, Shanghai Tower completes the ensemble of three supertall towers planned 25 years ago—a unified, triangular composition that includes the Jin Mao Tower and Shanghai World Financial Center. Together, they symbolize China's past, present, and future.

一个很中国的概念
A Very Chinese Idea

上海是我生长的城市，是个融合了世界各地的文化特色的城市。小时候，我的父母住在石库门，上海传统的老房子，而我的外祖父母则是住在前法租界，街道充满绿叶林荫。这是我小时候玩耍的地方。上海有很多有趣的层次，城市到处都藏着许多温馨的小地方。这种空间，让人就算离家很远，也可以感觉很自在。上海也有很多结合和缓冲室内室外的朦胧空间，这是一个很中国的概念。西方文化对于室内和室外的分隔是很明确的。上海人的日常起居大多是在室外，所以室外空间成为了住家的延伸。我希望上海中心能在超高层大楼中保留这种人性化空间的感觉，一个平静的空间，可以跟朋友碰面或是暂时抛下喧闹都市的地方。所以我们创造了垂直叠加的空中花园。

我们有时会猜想，上海中心往后会给世人留下什么样让人津津乐道的故事。大多数人关注的是大厦的高度，但对我来说，关键并不是做到最高，而是做到不负众望，最能适切的提供各种最佳的功能性。除此之外，我希望人们会记得上海中心的空中花园，对双层幕墙的独特运用，和将地面的水平社区垂直呈现的创意。我已期待多年，希望在完工的上海中心里，手里一杯咖啡，或读一本书，或和一位朋友愉快的谈天。现在，当我站在空中花园，我觉得这真的是一个非常上海的体验。

夏军
设计总监

Shanghai is my city—it has a unique cultural identity that blends influences from all parts of the world. My parents lived in a *shikumen*, a traditional lane house, and I spent a lot of time with my grandparents, who brought me up among the tree-lined streets of the French Concession. These are the places I played in as a child. Shanghai has so many interesting layers, with pockets of intimate space scattered everywhere. Even when you're not at home, you feel like you have personal space to enjoy. At the same time, all over the city there is a blending of inside and outside space, which is a very Chinese idea. Unlike in Western cultures, which separate inside from out, people in Shanghai live much of their lives outdoors and make outdoor spaces an extension of their homes. In the case of Shanghai Tower, I felt it was important to design a skyscraper that preserved that feeling of personal space—

a tranquil place to meet friends or find relief from the stress of the day. We did that by creating the sky gardens.

We sometimes speculate about the legacy of Shanghai Tower, which gets a lot of attention for its height. To me, the key is not to be the tallest, but to be the most responsible, be the most appropriate, and deliver the best possible performance. Beyond that, I hope we'll be remembered for the sky gardens, for the innovative double skin, and for exploring the possibilities of a vertical community that inspires people and elevates their lives. For years, I've been waiting to grab a cup of coffee, read a book, or strike up an interesting conversation high in the tower. Now when I go to the sky gardens, I feel like I'm having a very Shanghainese experience.

Jun Xia
Design Principal

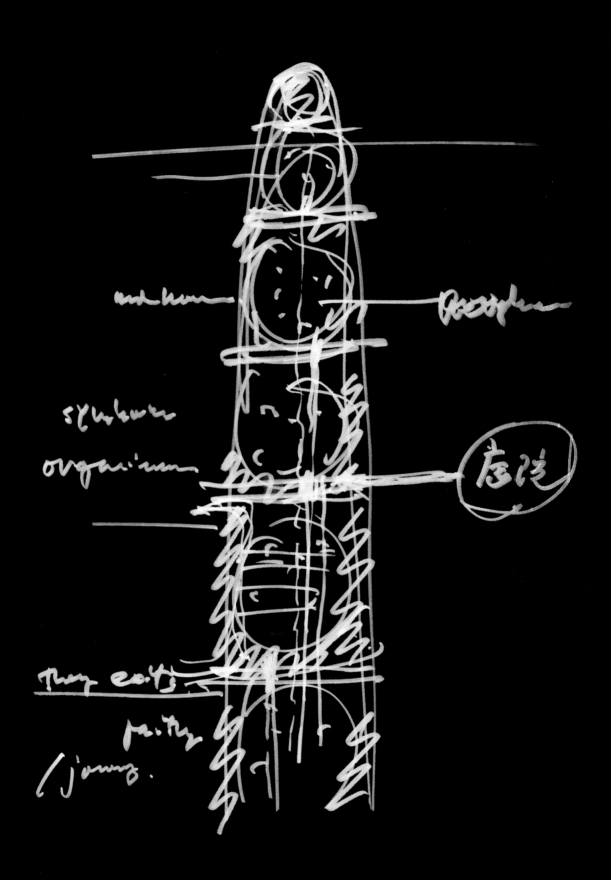

想象一个垂直建立的社区。

Just imagine a vertical community.

与自然相融

中国垂直建设的发展，追求的是与自然环境相融，天人合一，而不是为了战胜自然环境。上海中心大厦的螺旋形体，让建筑带有几何规律的缓缓自地面延伸向云端。而螺旋所隐喻的宇宙间轮回，正是万物生命的起源。螺旋也呼应原子的运动和结构，原子是最小的物理单位。

银河系最大的螺旋臂也是这个形体。另外，塔楼向上旋转攀升也象征着穿越时空，这是千百年来中国艺术、诗词、戏剧里常见的主题：向往天上仙境，以超越尘世的羁绊。

In harmony with nature

Building vertically in China has never been about dominating nature, but instead about striving to harmonize with nature, gradually ascending from earth to sky. The spiral form of Shanghai Tower makes that transition by lending a geometrical order to the tower and its reach toward the clouds. The spiral is a well-understood metaphor for the universal rotational force that is the basis of life.

It recalls both the form and motion of atoms, which are the smallest elements of physical matter, as well as the vast rotating arms of galaxies. In addition, the upward spiral represents movement through space and time, recalling a time-honored theme in Chinese art, poetry, and theater—the desire to transcend earthly preoccupations by connecting with the heavens.

超越尘世的羁绊。

Transcending earthly preoccupations.

顺着黄埔江的曲线，

Shaped by the river's curves,

上海中心与环境融为一体。

the tower respects its surroundings.

构筑
筑

Building the Dream

梦想

万丈高楼平地起

看着上海中心慢慢成型，是上海市民一直以来津津乐道的盛事。如此巨大的工程，需要庞大的人力。而由于上海市的土壤是典型河流三角洲松软的粘土地基，大厦必须在地下深植800多支钢筋混凝土巨柱来支撑建筑结构。六公尺（18英尺）深的大底板基础的浇筑过程非常壮观，大队混凝土车和大批工人团结合作，连续工作了两天半才顺利完成。

An epic journey

Watching the tower take shape has been an ongoing source of fascination and delight for the people of Shanghai. A source of national pride, the tower's construction was a colossal undertaking that required tremendous human effort. In a building of such rare scale, there were technical challenges, too.

Poor soil conditions in the city—a clay-based mixture typical of a river delta—meant supporting the tower on more than 800 reinforced concrete bore piles sunk deep into the ground. The pouring of the 6-meter-deep (18-foot) mat foundation was a great spectacle, with a fleet of trucks and a small army of workers on the job continuously for more than two and a half days.

每个月，上海中心的混凝土核心筒一段段完工，钢筋巨柱被吊起安置。机械兼避难层像树枝一般，从核心筒往外伸展，勾勒出大厦的圆三角基座和旋转的造型。

随着工程进行，每12-15层一区的大厦垂直分区渐渐成型。接着，用以支撑外层幕墙的外伸臂和环带桁架交织成网。最后，呈现上海中心大厦亮眼外观的玻璃幕墙也完成了。

Month by month, the tower rose as the concrete core grew higher and the gigantic steel sections for the supercolumns were hoisted in place. The mechanical/refuge floors, extending outward from the cylindrical tower like branches of a tree, began to suggest the triangular footprint and twist of the building.

As progress continued, the division of the tower into vertical zones, each 12 to 15 stories tall, became clearly apparent. Then new layers appeared—the lattice-work of steel to support the outer skin and, ultimately, the glass enclosure that gives the tower its recognizable profile.

工人同心协力。

Built by determined workers.

充满期待的开端。

Beginnings filled with anticipation.

47

大批的工人

A community of workers

日复一日在工地聚集。

gathered each day to begin again.

庞然巨柱支撑起大厦。

Strengthened by massive supercolumns.

一区一区，拔地而起。

The tower rose higher, zone by zone.

捕捉风的能量。

Harnessing the power of wind.

经年累月的努力，

After years of progress,

天际线上的新亮点终于成型。

a new presence on the skyline.

裙楼

Ground, Skin, and Sky

幕墙和

塔冠

从地面到云端

上海中心大厦反映了浦东区的快速转型。
短短的25年间，原本的矮房、厂房和稻田
已经被深具影响力的全球金融中心取代，
而上海中心大厦正是陆家嘴金融大厦群
的画龙点睛之作。

大厦本身就是个社交聚集地，可以同时容纳
三万人。它以公园、广场、街道、人行步道和
公共交通与城市的脉动联成一气。底层的
裙楼出入口兼聚集地，迎接人群进入一个
非常上海的综合体大楼。

From earth to sky

Shanghai Tower embodies the dramatic
transformation of the city's Pudong
district. In little more than a quarter-
century, a low-rise district of prosaic
factories, warehouses, and rice fields
has developed into a high-powered
global financial center, with Shanghai
Tower as the unifying landmark.

The tower is a community in itself, able
to accommodate a population of 30,000
people at a time. It engages the city
through the connective tissue of parks,
plazas, streets, sidewalks, and transit.
The lower-level podium is the entry
and gathering place, the threshold to a
mixed-use tower whose characteristics
are quintessential Shanghai.

裙楼之上，独创的双层玻璃幕墙向上盘旋，围绕着上海中心独有的21个空中花园，这是全球前所未见的。采光良好的中庭像城市里的广场一般，人们可以在此聚集。空中花园楼层的商店和餐厅为大楼的使用者提供一个可以和亲友聚会的空间。

高耸入天际的塔冠，象征着上海跃升为全球大都市的峥嵘地位。塔冠里的观景台有三层楼，是家喻户晓的上海地标，可将上海的景观尽收眼底，或到屋顶参观风力发电机。

Rising above the podium, the spiral form of the tower is achieved through an inventive double skin that encloses 21 sky gardens, the first of their kind. These light-filled atria serve much as plazas and squares do, bringing people together in places that everyone shares. Shops and restaurants on these levels will offer destinations where people mix with friends and family.

The tower touches the sky with a soaring crown, whose upward thrust symbolizes the city's ascension as a global metropolis. It is a coveted destination, with three observation levels that open to panoramic views of the city and offer rooftop access among power-generating wind turbines.

缓缓盘旋入天际的上海新地标。

An icon, spiraling toward the sky.

裙楼、大厦、塔冠——

Podium, tower, and crown—

上海都会生活新核心。

new centers of urban life.

裙楼
Ground

上海中心大厦是一个独特的地标，对来到陆家嘴的旅客、购物人潮、上班族、参加会议的来宾和酒店房客而言，它既是个门户也是个枢纽。地面的商业裙楼别具一格的铸造玻璃外墙光彩夺目。耀眼的裙楼内除了商店和餐厅外，还有一个多功能会议中心，是

黄浦江以东最大的展演场地，可以吸引更多音乐会、表演节目、艺术展览以及社交活动到这个区块。对于近年来快速发展为亚洲最受瞩目的陆家嘴金融贸易区来说，上海中心大厦是一个重要枢纽。

Both gateway and connector, Shanghai Tower is a destination for people from all walks of life: tourists, shoppers, office workers, meeting attendees, and hotel guests in the Lujiazui commercial zone. They come from all corners of the world. The building meets the ground with its distinctive podium, clad in luminous cast-glass tiles.

In addition to shops and restaurants, the podium houses a conference center whose multifunction hall—the largest gathering space in the zone east of the Huangpu River—will attract audiences to concerts, performances, art exhibits, and social events. The tower is a new crossroads in Pudong, a quarter of the city that has emerged as one of Asia's most recognizable super-highrise precincts.

每天都有数千人来到上海中心，经过绿化的广场或是地下通道，直接连接来自地下转运站的通勤人潮。大厅的功能类似一个社区市集，人们可以在回家路上顺道买点东西。在五层楼高的中庭内，可以看到楼上的商店。

宽广的玻璃外墙，将室内和室外空间作了视觉连接。地面楼层有两座精心设计的明亮大厅，一座供酒店房客和参加会议的来宾使用，另一座则通往办公楼层，这给上海中心大厦提供了多用途的出入口，通往作为大厦垂直通道的各个电梯。

Thousands of people arrive at the tower each day through the landscaped plazas or from below ground, with tunnels that feed commuters directly into the lower levels from an adjacent transit station. The concourse has the feel of a neighborhood marketplace, where people can conveniently pick up items on the way home after work.

Inside the five-story atrium, they can also glimpse the retail stores above. The atrium's expansive glass façade opens toward the city, making an important visual connection. At street level, two light-filled, dedicated lobbies—one for hotel and conference patrons and the other for office workers—provide additional entrances to the tower and access elevators that are its vertical arteries.

空中社区的梦想。

The dream of a community in the sky.

幕墙
Skin

上海中心外型线条看似简单利落，但是双层幕墙建筑的设计、工程、制造和安装复杂度实际上相当的高。项目设计团队透过多次的风洞实验，以确定上海中心能抵抗这个区域破坏力最强的自然现象：台风。

在试过多种方案后，团队抓住了最完美的旋转角度，可以最大幅度的降低风载，同时不失去外观的美感。参数化设计技术让团队能深入研究微调不同的立面方案，精准规划两万多面幕墙组合，制造七千种不同规格的玻璃面板。

The elegant simplicity of the tower's signature profile masks the complexity that underlies its design, engineering, fabrication, and assembly. To refine the tower's shape, the design team conducted a battery of wind tunnel tests to simulate the region's greatest destructive force, the typhoon.

Many alternatives were tested to determine the optimal rotation for the tower's spiral design, one that would minimize wind loads while achieving a compelling form. The emergence of parametric design platforms enabled the team to study many configurations for the outer skin, which includes more than 20,000 curtain wall panels—and some 7,000 unique shapes.

不同于传统建筑从地面往上筑墙, 上海中心大厦的玻璃外墙是分别在各层分区由上往下建成的。独特的悬臂吊挂着铁杆的外墙系统, 克服了一个极大的设计挑战。V字形的凹槽凸显了外墙的螺旋几何形体, 同时缓减了建筑周边的风力。

最后, 上海中心透明的第二层玻璃幕墙, 创造出独一无二的空中花园。它所提供的空间感和社交体验使得上海中心得以傲视群厦, 与其他超高建筑有所不同。

Unlike a more conventional building, in which the walls are built from the ground up, the outer glass wall of Shanghai Tower was most efficiently constructed from the top down within each zone. A system of rods and cables suspended from above solved a difficult design challenge. On the exterior, a deep V-notch in the façade makes the spiraling geometry readily apparent, while deflecting the winds that swirl around the building. Ultimately, it is the tower's transparent second skin that creates the possibility for the one-of-a-kind sky gardens. They provide a spatial and social experience that distinguishes Shanghai Tower from any other highrise.

自然光充满着空中花园。

Sunlight fills the sky gardens.

前所未有的空间体验。

A spatial experience unlike any other.

上海中心利落的外型

The tower's elegant profile

隐藏了设计的复杂性。

masks the complexity of its design.

超越时空的形体。

A form that transcends time and space.

上海再次成为全球中心。

Shanghai's re-emergence as a global center.

塔冠
Sky

上海中心最与众不同的是它独特的轮廓，盘旋的玻璃塔冠高耸入云，象征着上海跃升为一座国际化的金融首都。九个分区中最高的塔冠里，有着可以享受无敌景观的公共空间，并展示超高层建筑永续发展科技的日常运用。

全世界最快的高速电梯，一分钟就可以飞快地将访客送达顶楼与世隔绝的观景台。在这里有餐厅和咖啡厅，提供优雅舒适的享受。最值得一提的独特体验，是121楼的开放式观景台，在这里访客可以参观一排排提供大楼部分照明电力的风力发电机。

One of the most distinguishing aspects of Shanghai Tower is its unique silhouette, which meets the sky with a twisting glass crown. Its upward trajectory symbolizes Shanghai's rise to prominence as an international business capital. The crown—the highest of the tower's nine zones—houses public spaces that enjoy unmatched views of the city and demonstrate ways that sustainable technologies can be an everyday part of highrise buildings. In a minute's time, high-speed elevators—the world's fastest—whisk visitors to enclosed observation platforms on the uppermost floors.

在最顶层的平台，游客可以亲眼目睹壮观的重量级阻尼器，这座1000公吨重的阻尼器由钢板组成，以钢筋悬挂着。

阻尼器可以减缓塔楼的摇晃，减少高楼内使用者的不适。这个展区里的最后的亮点，是一座现代雕塑，会随着阻尼器的晃动而摇摆。

Amenities also include a restaurant, café, and, on the 121st floor, the most unique experience of all: an open-air observation deck. There, visitors can walk on the rooftop, surrounded by the rows of wind turbines that generate power to illuminate parts of the tower. On a platform above, people marvel at the massive tuned mass damper—

a 1,000-metric-ton (1,100-ton) assembly of steel plates suspended by thick steel cables. The damper slows the swaying of the tower, improving the comfort of occupants. The focal point of the gallery is a contemporary sculpture, which glides with the back-and-forth movements of the counterweight.

天际线上独有的轮廓。

A distinctive silhouette on the skyline.

人人向往的空中地标，

A coveted destination

个个难忘的空间体验。

and a memorable experience.

顶天立地。

A connection between heaven and earth.

成就一世界之

Impacting a World City

擎天巨塔登场

上海中心耀眼的外形不仅提供了上海市民无限的想象空间，也给全世界的人带来启发。从它和谐的比例到它旋转向上的形式，都传达了美感和积极向上的乐观。上海中心大厦吸引市民广大关注，大家纷纷把在日常生活中观察到的上海中心，透过图片视频在社群网站上分享。

这座上海天际线上的高耸地标，在上海每个角落都能看得到。它诉说着上海在世界上举足轻重的地位，转型成一个亮眼的国际化大都会，让上海市民对自己、这个城市和国家的卓越成就感到骄傲。

A towering presence

Shanghai Tower's shimmering form has captured the imagination of people across the city and around the world. Everything about it, from its proportions to its winding form, conveys beauty and optimism alike. Its presence radiates across the community, registered by people as they experience it in the course of their daily lives and shared continuously through the images they post on social media.

A soaring icon on the city skyline, the tower is visible for miles in the distance. It speaks to Shanghai's place in the world, to its transformation as a global metropolis, and to the pride of its citizens in what the city and the nation have accomplished.

这是第一座由本地团队领军设计开发的超高层大厦，而不是单纯仰赖外来资金和设计。由于上海中心许多的设计元素来自城市提供的独特灵感，上海人对它特别有认同感。

上海中心是一个艺术杰作，是一个技术创新的成果，也是来自人性最精巧的设计。它不只是一座建筑物，更是一个照亮天际的地标，时时提醒大家上海在中国和在全世界如日中天的地位。

People are quick to acknowledge that this is the first of Shanghai's supertall towers to be designed and developed locally, rather than with capital and talent from abroad. Given that so many of the tower's design elements are uniquely inspired by Shanghai, people of the city have a strong sense of ownership.

Shanghai Tower is art, it is science, it is design, and it is human ingenuity—not simply architecture, but a landmark that lights up the sky and reminds the city of its rising position in China and the world.

构筑一个社区
Building Community

上海中心是一座世界级的建筑，却不可或缺地承载着当地团队的卓越贡献。我们在上海的同仁了解当地的实践，熟悉当地的法规和建设程序。同时，上海的团队确证了上海中心是中国文化和生活方式的真实反映，特别是适切地将上海石库门邻里文化融入到上海中心的设计中。这是一个全球关注的项目，但是除了上海，没有别的地方更适合这样的设计。上海中心大厦通过规划和建筑的语汇展示着当地的传统和文化的精髓，传承并赋之予能量。

上海中心大厦的三维设计理念，使得它区别于其他的超高层建筑，并如大树生根般稳固地屹立着。上海中心是真实的多重社区的写照，相互堆叠上升。最关键的是着眼于人们如何在这个空间工作和生活，他们需要的服务和支持，所享有的高品质生活体验—既放眼未来，同时缅怀过去。在设计上海中心时，我们用了不同的思维方式来构筑一个社区。我们仔细思索关于垂直城市，多功能用途的平衡，以及开放性与私密性的兼顾等基本概念。创建一个有生命力的城市环境并不会只因一座超高层大楼的凭空而降而产生。建筑和空间需要相互联系。我们需持续关注垂直城市，并且用三维的模式构筑立体的都市空间。上海中心大厦的设计便是在这样的思维下，迈出了一大步。它为超高层建筑设计的因地制宜和以人为本提供了新想法。

李晓梅
项目总监

Shanghai Tower is a world-class building, but it wouldn't be the same without the contributions of the local team in China. Our people in Shanghai understand local practices, we're experienced with the codes and regulatory agencies, and we know how to navigate the approvals process. In this case, the local team also ensured that the tower is an authentic reflection of Chinese culture and lifestyles, particularly in its interpretation of the Shanghainese *shikumen* neighborhood culture. This project is of global interest, but it would not be a good fit just anywhere in the world. The DNA of Shanghai Tower is extracted from the local culture and heritage, and then translated into the planning and architecture of the building without losing its energy.

It's the planning aspects of Shanghai Tower—three-dimensional planning—that distinguish it most from other supertall buildings and root it firmly in place. The tower is really about multiple communities stacked on top of each other. The focal point is how people work and live in the space, what services they need for support, and the quality of the experience—looking forward and also back to history. In designing this building, we followed a different road map. We explored fundamental concepts about vertical cities, the balance of mixed uses, openness, and inclusivity. You can't just drop a highrise down in a city and create a viable urban environment. Buildings and spaces need to be interconnected. We need to keep looking at vertical urbanism and start modeling cities in three dimensions. Shanghai Tower is a big step in that direction. It offers new ideas for how tall buildings can be place-based and people-centered.

Xiaomei Lee
Project Director

上海给的灵感，

Inspired by Shanghai

市民给的力量。

and embraced by her people.

一柱擎天的地标，远近都能见到。

A towering icon, experienced near and far.

展现出城市的能量

Reflecting the city's energy

象征着上海的骄傲。

and symbolizing its pride.

缅怀过去，

Recalling the city's history

放眼未来。

and pointing to its future.

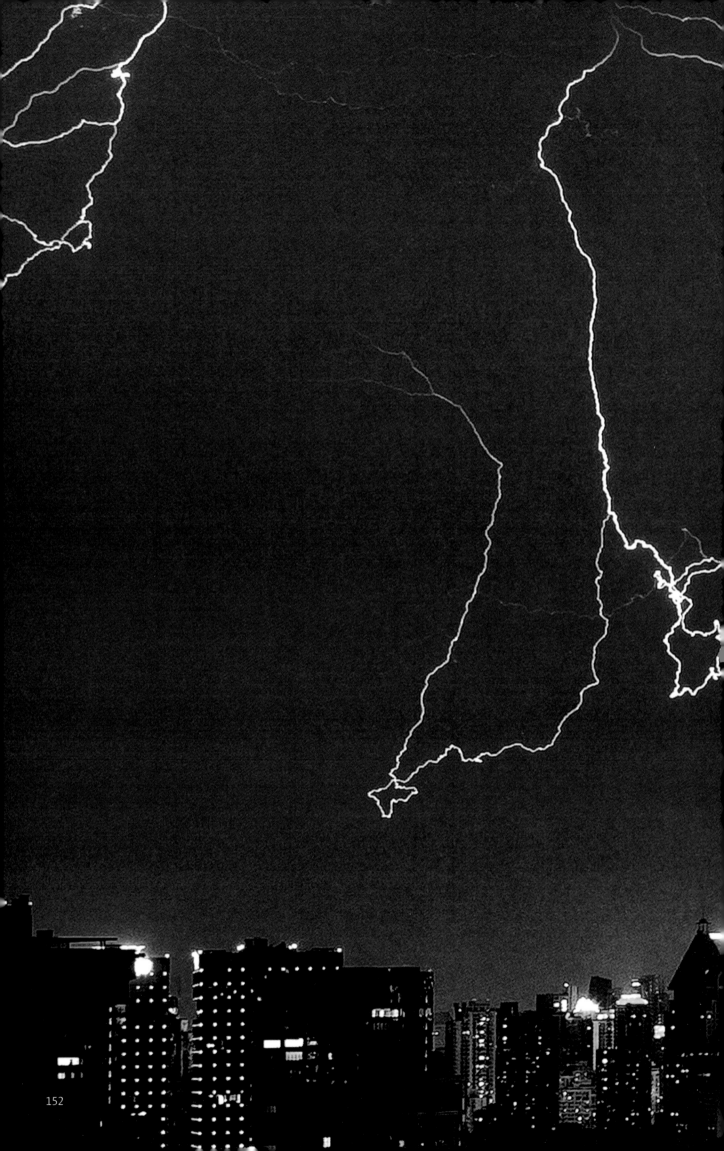

捕捉上海市的想象力，

Capturing the city's imagination

留下深刻上海印象。

and making lasting impressions.

上海中
设计团

Shanghai Tower's Team

心队

全球团队合作

上海中心大厦的完工，得归功于一路以来辛勤付出的团队成员，也要感谢上海这个独特的城市，上海市民，以及多年来同心协力的工人团队成就了这样的项目。上海中心的设计和建造是一个非常庞大的工程，跨越了八年的时间，动员了Gensler各个不同部门专业团队以及全球顶尖的顾问专家。

上海中心大厦最早的设计发想始于2006年，上海中心大厦建设发展有限公司宣布举行国际设计竞标时开始的。Gensler常年的设计顾问伙伴，从结构、机械、景观到电梯顾问公司，各个马上就位，蓄势待发。另一个重要的合作伙伴是同济大学建筑设计研究院集团，驻上海的技术顾问团队。

A global accomplishment

Shanghai Tower can be credited to a team of the most extraordinary people in the world—touched by the city, its residents, and the legion of dedicated workers. The design and construction of the tower, in particular, was an immense undertaking, spanning more than eight years and involving a diverse team of Gensler professionals and consulting partners worldwide.

Ideation for the building began in 2006, when Shanghai Tower Construction & Development Co., Ltd., announced an international design competition for the tower. Our partners in the design—structural and mechanical engineers, landscape architects, and elevator consultants—came on board immediately. Another key collaborator was the local architect of record, Tongji Architectural Design Group.

Gensler内部则动员了全球在建筑、室内、商业和品牌设计等各个领域的专家，组成了一个核心团队。我们也集合了永续发展、幕墙设计和交通等技术专家。上海中心大厦的规模和复杂性在中国的建筑史上创造了许多个"第一"。

为了分析关键设计，我们成立了上百个专家研究小组，来探讨如何执行关键的设计节点。上海中心大厦相当于是重写了新的建筑规章，中国和上海市政府都有参与讨论对话，对于许多设计决策是至关重要的。

Internally, Gensler mobilized a core group from its global network, tapping specialists in areas such as architecture, interiors, retail, and branding. We assembled in-house technical experts in sustainability, curtain wall design, and transportation. The tower's scale and complexity created so many "firsts" for China's construction industry that more than 100 expert panels were established to analyze key aspects of the design. In a sense, we had to write building codes that didn't exist. The highest bodies in the Chinese and Shanghai governments were represented, and this dialogue was critical in finalizing many design decisions.

非凡的成就，

An extraordinary accomplishment,

来自尽心尽力的专业团队。

shared by a dedicated team.

一个当地的团队，一个全球的团队
A Local Team, a Global Team

毋庸置疑的，上海中心大厦对Gensler来说是个突破性的项目。在赢得这项国际设计比赛之前，我们从未设计过这种规模的项目。但Gensler在机场、大型竞技场、都市规划等领域有丰富经验，使得我们对于人群在城市中或是大型建筑物里的体验和互动有深度了解。上海中心让我们有机会向世界证明我们能处理高复杂度的大规模建筑项目。

上海中心项目由Gensler上海当地团队统筹，同时也动用了许多各地办公室的资源，尤其是美国芝加哥、旧金山、洛杉矶和休斯敦。从项目初始，我们就坚持打造一个国际化的团队，结合Gensler各地专家的特长，也在上海当地雇用新成员。上海中心是个跨地区，全公司总动员的项目，核心项目团队有将近

九十位来自各个领域的专家，包括建筑、室内、品牌和平面设计。

我们设计上海中心的方式，完全反映了Gensler全球一体化的企业文化。这般规模的项目需要我们从世界各地的办公室挖掘出最称职的设计专家。夏军是我合作多年的伙伴，也是个相当了不起的设计师，他把上海地道文化直接带进了公司大门，我非常感激他的独到视野和领导智慧。但是最终的功劳还是全公司共享的，多亏了公司成员团队合作、群星睿智的文化，才能成就这栋体现团队视野和贡献的伟大建筑。

Dan Winey
执行总监

There's no debating that Shanghai Tower is a landmark project for our firm. Prior to winning this international competition, we had never designed a building of this scale and complexity. But our expertise in dealing with airports and stadiums, and also urban design, has taught us a lot about how people experience large buildings and navigate cities. This was an opportunity to show how well we can handle the biggest and most complex projects in the world.

This project was fully managed by our people in Shanghai, but we also used resources at a number of our offices—most notably in Chicago, San Francisco, Los Angeles, and Houston. From the beginning, we made a commitment to build a truly international team, combining Gensler specialists from around the world and hiring local staff as well. It really was an effort of the entire firm, involving a

core team of almost 90 professionals with a wide range of expertise, including architecture, interiors, landscape, and graphic design.

The way we approached the tower is reflective of our "one-firm firm" culture. A project of this scale demands that we identify and leverage extraordinary talent. My partner, Jun Xia, is an amazing designer who brought the culture of Shanghai straight to our doorstep. I'm eternally grateful for his insight and wisdom. But it really is the firm's accomplishment—acknowledging that we work using a collaborative process. We believe in a constellation of stars, and this building is proof of the entire team's vision and dedication.

Dan Winey
Executive Principal

由上海团队带头，

Led by our people in Shanghai,

集合全球专家的智慧。

supported from around the world.

项目里程碑
Key Milestones

2008

Gensler 赢得项目

Gensler方案赢得国际设计竞标
项目开始进行。

四月:	宣布Gensler为设计顾问
五月:	设计团队组成
六月:	方案设计开始
十一月:	破土动工

2009

设计工作继续进行

专家团队陆续审核建筑设计文件。

二月:	最后一轮风洞测试
四月:	扩初设计完成
六月:	连续墙浇筑
七月:	结构专家团队集合
七月:	生命安全专家团队集合
九月:	塔楼招标文件完成
十月:	幕墙招标文件完成

Competition Win

Gensler wins international design
competition and work commences.

April:	Gensler win announced
May:	Design teams assigned
June:	Schematic design begins
Nov:	Groundbreaking

Design Moves Ahead

Design documents progress as expert
panels review the tower's plans.

Feb:	Final wind tunnel test
April:	Design development completed
June:	Slurry wall poured
July:	Structural expert panel convened
July:	Life safety expert panel convened
Sept:	Tower tender package completed
Oct:	Curtain wall tender package completed

2010

基础浇筑

大底板到位，钢筋巨柱立起。

三月：　大底板桩基浇筑
四月：　公共空间室内设计招标
　　　　文件完成
九月：　初步结构基础到位
十月：　得到建造证书和许可证

2011

核心筒和外壳

钢筋结构逐渐成型。

六月：　施工达到第一百米里程碑
十一月：塔冠方案文件完成
十二月：施工高度达到200米

Foundation Poured

Massive foundation goes into
place; supercolumns emerge
from the ground.

March:　Mat foundation poured
April:　Common area interiors tender
　　　　package completed
Sept:　First structural elements are
　　　　placed on foundation
Oct:　　Certificates and permits issued

Core and Shell Rise

Steel superstructure takes
recognizable form.

June:　Construction reaches
　　　　first 100-meter milestone
Nov:　Crown optimization
　　　　package completed
Dec:　Construction reaches 200
　　　　meters

项目里程碑
Key Milestones

2012

超高层塔楼成型

建筑高度超过400米，外层幕墙
陆续完成。

五月：　　建筑高度到达300米
七月：　　裙楼东面钢结构完成
八月：　　裙楼西面钢结构完成
八月：　　裙楼西面外幕墙开始施工
十一月：　二区幕墙完工
十二月：　建筑高度达到400米

A Skyscraper Emerges

Building height exceeds 400 meters
and outer skin advances higher.

May:　　　Construction reaches
　　　　　300 meters
July:　　　East podium steel
　　　　　structure installed
Aug:　　　West podium steel
　　　　　structure installed
Aug:　　　Outer curtain wall
　　　　　installation begins
Nov:　　　Zone 2 curtain wall completed
Dec:　　　Construction reaches
　　　　　400 meters

2013

封顶

隆重庆祝楼顶梁柱和主要
钢筋结构完成。

二月：　　三区幕墙完成
四月：　　施工高度达到500米
五月：　　四区幕墙完成
八月：　　主体结构封顶
九月：　　五区幕墙完成
十一月：　六区幕墙完成

Topping Out

Celebration marks placement of
topmost beam as main steel structure
is completed.

Feb:　　　Zone 3 curtain wall completed
April:　　Construction reaches
　　　　　500 meters
May:　　　Zone 4 curtain wall completed
Aug:　　　Topping out of main structure
Sept:　　Zone 5 curtain wall completed
Nov:　　　Zone 6 curtain wall completed

2014

塔冠

塔楼顶终于在城市天际线上成型。

一月： 建筑高度达到600米
一月： 阻尼器安装完成
一月： 七区幕墙完成
六月： 八区幕墙完成
八月： 塔冠达到632米
十一月： 塔冠幕墙完成

Crowning

Apex of the tower takes final
shape on the city skyline.

Jan: Construction reaches
 600 meters
Jan: Tuned mass damper installed
Jan: Zone 7 curtain wall completed
June: Zone 8 curtain wall completed
Aug: Crown reaches high point
 of 632 meters
Nov: Crown curtain wall completed

2015

大功告成

大堂完工，景观绿化，塔楼陆续开放。

一月： 裙楼幕墙完工
四月： 公共大堂和景观工程完成
秋季： 上海中心大厦正式开幕

Finishing Touches

Team completes lobbies, installs
landscaping, and opens tower to visitors.

Jan: Podium curtain wall completed
April: Public lobbies and site
 landscaping completed
Fall: Shanghai Tower opens

项目信息
Building Facts

地理位置

地点: 中国上海浦东新区陆家嘴
金融贸易区

面积: 30,370平方米

塔楼

高度: 632米（2,073英尺）

楼层: 121可用楼层

面积: 地上面积41万平方米，
地下面积16.6万平方米

功能: 办公、豪华酒店、娱乐、观光、
零售、餐饮和文化场所

裙楼

高度: 36.9米

楼层: 地上5层

面积: 46,000平方米

功能: 零售、银行、餐厅、会展和
宴会。地下楼层有零售，
1,950个停车位、服务和机电
配套功能。

Site

Location: Lujiazui Finance and Trade
Zone, Pudong district,
Shanghai, China

Area: 30,370 square meters
(7.5 acres)

Tower

Height: 632 meters (2,073 ft)

Stories: 121 occupied floors

Area: 410,000 square meters
above grade (4.4M sf)
166,000 square meters
below grade (1.8M sf)

Program: Office, luxury hotel,
entertainment, retail,
food and beverage, and
cultural venues

Podium

Height: 36.9 meters (121 ft)

Stories: 5 stories above grade

Area: 46,000 square meters
(495,000 sf)

Program: Retail, banking, restaurant,
conference, meeting, and
banquet functions. Below-
grade levels house retail,
1,950 parking spaces, service,
and MEP functions.

团队信息
Project Credits and Consultants

Owner and Developer
Shanghai Tower Construction &
Development Co., Ltd.
Shanghai, China

Contractor
Shanghai Construction Group
Shanghai, China

Design Architects
Gensler
San Francisco, California

Local Design Institute
Tongji Architectural Design Group
Shanghai, China

Structural Engineers
Thornton Tomasetti
New York, New York

Landscape Architects
SWA
Sausalito, California

MEP Engineers
Cosentini Associates
New York, New York

Fire/Life Safety
Jensen Hughes (formerly Rolf Jensen &
Associates International, Inc.)
Baltimore, Maryland

Elevators
Edgett Williams Consulting Group
Mill Valley, California

Façade Consultant
Aurecon
Melbourne, Australia

Wind Engineers
RWDI
Guelph, Ontario

Specialty Lighting
PHA Lighting Design, Inc.
Atlanta, Georgia

Building Maintenance Systems
HighRise Systems, Inc.
Grand Prairie, Texas

Wind Engineering Peer Review
BLWTL/UWO
London, Ontario

Parking and Traffic
Walker Parking Consultants
San Francisco, California

Geotechnical Peer Review
STS, Inc.
Chicago, Illinois

Cost Estimating
Shanghai Shenyuan Property Consultants
Shanghai, China

Geothermal Design
koopX
Berlin, Germany

Light Pollution
Shanghai Academy of
Environmental Sciences
Shanghai, China

业主兼开发商
上海中心大厦建设开发有限公司
中国·上海

施工承包
上海建工集团股份有限公司
中国·上海

建筑设计
Gensler
美国·加州旧金山

当地设计院
同济大学建筑设计研究院
中国·上海

结构工程
美国宋腾汤玛沙帝结构师事务所
美国·纽约

景观建筑
SWA 事务所
美国·加州索萨利托

机电工程
柯森提尼联合工程设计公司
美国·纽约

生命安全
Jensen Hughes（原 Rolf Jensen &
Associates International, Inc.）
美国·巴尔的摩

垂直交通
Edgett Williams Consulting Group
美国·加州米尔谷

幕墙顾问
澳昱冠
澳大利亚·墨尔本

风力工程
RWDI
加拿大·安大略省贵湖

特殊灯光
PHA Lighting Design, Inc.
美国·乔治亚州亚特兰大

建筑维护系统
HighRise Systems, Inc.
美国·德州大草原城

风力工程同行审查
BLWTL/UWO
加拿大·安大略省伦敦

泊车和交通
Walker Parking Consultants
美国·旧金山

土木工程同行审查
STS, Inc.
美国·伊利诺州芝加哥

成本估算
上海申元工程投资咨询有限公司
中国·上海

地热设计
koopX
德国·柏林

光污染
上海市环境科学研究院
中国·上海

Gensler 团队
The Gensler Team

Beijing
Zheng Xiang 向征

Chicago
Jorge Barrero
Mike Concannon
Dick Fencl
Tim Jacobson
Andrew Senderak
Hyun Tak 卓炫铭
Grant Uhlir
Aleksandar Sasha Zeljic

Detroit
Randall Reeves

Houston
Roland Garza
Lisa Graiff
Winnie Law 罗咏怡
Suzanne Schreider
Marshall Strabala
Andrew Sutton

Los Angeles
John Circenis
Andy Cohen
Robert Garlipp
David Glover
Clara Kim
Bart Tucker

San Francisco
Jonathan Beard
Dian Duvall
Art Gensler Jr.
Tom Horton
Chu-Jun Huang
Tim Huey
Frederick Liu 廖世荣
Mark McMinn
Kenneth Rasco
George Slavik
Ben Tranel
Bob Wheatley
Dan Winey

Shanghai
Christopher Chan 陈国荣
Jean Chen 陈德瑾
Min Chu 朱旼
Abby DeWolfe
Howe Keen Foong 冯皓镜
Cathy Gu 顾志红
Evan Gu 顾锷
Angela Han 韩琪
Hui-Ling Hsieh 谢蕙龄
Linn Hu 胡靓
Ken Huang 黄国钦
Sam Huang 黄帅
Xiaomei Lee 李晓梅
Rudy Letsche III
Flora Li 李晓红
Dongxiao Liu 刘冬晓
Armando Lopez
Junjie Ma 马君杰
Callum MacBean
Ted Nordstrom
Patrick Owens

Christine Peng 彭媛媛
Michael Peng 彭武
Kamol Prateepmanowong
Robert Price
Freck Qin 秦振晖
Tadeusz Rajwer
Sophie Reid
Nancy Shen 沈茜
Rainy Shen 沈雨薇
Jue Shi 石珏
Ray Shick
Julia Song 宋佳丽
Zhipeng Sun 孙志鹏
Zia Tyebjee
Chun Wang 王春
Cindy Wang 王辛
Linn Wang 王桂林
Eliza Wong 王慧思
Cloud Wu 吴云
Jun Xia 夏军
Tina Yang 杨延青
Jeff Yu 游原嵩
Meizi Zeng 曾美子
Qiao Zhang 张樵
Shengtao Zhang 张圣涛
Aidong Zheng 郑爱东
Liming Zhou 周立明
Shimiao Zhou 周诗邈
Cloud Zhu 朱蕴盛

Tokyo
Jeffrey Halverson

Washington DC
Gabriel Lopez
Bea de Paz
Tanja Speckmann

180

照 片 来 源
Image Credits